HANNAH'S TRAVEL
by
Richard Speakes

Ahsahta Press

Boise State University
Boise, Idaho

These poems have appeared in the following magazines:

The Iowa Review: "The fathers," "Evidence," "Sara," "Making ready," "My father 3 days before we leave," "The preacher at St. Joe," "Seeing my sister," "June 9, 1852," and "At Ft. Laramie."
The Seattle Review: "Portents," "January 2, 1852," "June 5, 1852," "June 13, 1852," and "June 21, 1852."

Editor for Ahsahta Press: Tom Trusky

ISBN 0-916272-19-2

Library of Congress Catalog Card Number:
81-71243

for Richard Blessing

Judy Appel, Richard Blessing, Kate McCune, and William Matthews gave me helpful criticisms (and plain help) while I was writing these poems; I thank them.

Contents

Introduction

Richard Speakes has written a tour de force: a book of linked poems, in narrative sequence, set in 1851 and 1852 between Macune, Missouri, and Ft. Laramie, and thought, spoken, and daydreamed by a woman, Speakes' arresting heroine Hannah. The enterprise itself is enough to draw our attention, but what holds it is an uncommon achievement in poetry—the creation of a complex and compelling character who is importantly other than the poet. Not a persona, but a character.

An equally important achievement, nearly as rare, is the discovery, again and again, of a balance between the urge individual poems develop to behave like single, self-sufficient lyric poems on the one hand, and on the other the need the book has to be one long structure less intensely concentrated than a lyric poem but never less interesting on its surface, line by line and poem by poem.

American poetry has a great poem, John Berryman's **Homage To Mistress Bradstreet** (1956), which is historical, is a linked sequence of individual poems with a narrative, and is thought, spoken, and day-dreamed by a woman. There is one important way it is unfair to compare them: Speakes has written his poem at the beginning of his poetic maturity, and Berryman wrote his at the beginning of his mastery. But we should perhaps note that this early in his writing life Speakes has written a poem so difficult and ambitious—perhaps to try such a thing one needs not to know very well what one can and can't do, for if one does it might all seem forfeit in advance—that it is hard to find another book to compare it to other than Berryman's startling masterpiece. I can think of another way they might be spoken of similarly. Some will think it a remarkable feat for Speakes to have spoken so believably in the voice of a woman. This is no small triumph for him, but in thinking of it we would do well to remember how thoroughly in our century poetry asks poets to write down not what was oft thought but ne'er so well expressed, but what the poet couldn't have said without the challenge and process of the poem. We ask our poets not to be limited to or by themselves, but to live in the sympathetic imagination, and we might say matter-of-factly about Speakes' fine book that, evidently, he thought that was not too much to ask.

Berryman had the advantage of a heroine who was also a poet, and a poet in a cheerfully more rhetorical age than ours. Speakes has a heroine who knows the Bible a little, trusts the evidence of her senses, and had the good fortune to be invented by Speakes. And so she is a woman who, entering pregnancy and soon after that the long trek westward, can say to herself:

What is strange is in my arms.

The men with whom she will set out tell stories about what they hope and fear to find:

> They were like a boy
> throwing a ball against the barn at dusk,
> & in the failing light the body's lamp
> reaches to where the catch will be.

The syntax is a tiny bit formal to our ears—this conveys both a sense of an earlier colloquial range and of the formality used by a verbal person without a verbal education to match her natural talent. The ampersand is a winning touch; it suggests not only the shorthand of journal entries but also the conventions of printing from which Hannah's unbookish formality is both not so far and far.

Another example of Speakes' exact sense of tact illustrates how it operates over the length of a whole poem—the one dated "June 15, 1852"—and how what it registers (rises and dips in how "formal" diction is, for example) is the process of thought itself. Hannah is thinking about her husband, who has killed a buffalo:

> The fortress of his dream
> is the world as it relents
> to his impressions
> & holds them for a spell—
> wagon tracks, a mound of earth
> & it the cross, the scar
> across his stronger hand—
> earnings in the tender
> of arrival.
>   Why else lug
> the bison's head & raise it
> by its horns, but that it reminds
> his desire is substantial—
> & didn't the creature run
> as if it knew his mind?
> Good or bad makes no matter,
> instead it all has meaning—
> a stronghold of such size
> one can't tell if more's
> held out or in.

There is almost more here, in the poem as well as in **Hannah's Travel**, than Speakes can handle—her theological and hymn-diction puns lead her continually toward dense philosophical problems. But how pleasing it is to see him take on so much. So it's not surprising, after all, that his moving and readable book reminds us of the work of such accomplished poets as Berryman, Margaret Atwood (**The Journals of Susannah Moody**) and George Keithley (**The Donner Party**). His future is one to watch, and **Hannah's Travel** is a book to read and re-read.

William Matthews
Seattle, Washington
January, 1982

The fathers

May 3, 1851
Macune, Missouri

They recede from here like straight fence
that gives the land both sides,
like the bodies of men who settled
Missouri, Kentucky, western Virginia.
As young men, each one saw the land
left to him, & every time he looked
he heard all its stories, the early frost
& luck of rain, the child who died
& his own fever passing.
                              One night John leans
against the table whose every mark is the light
it was made in, his father glaring out
at weather, making the boy feel like weather.
When it lifts in the sky the father thinks
the boy's soaring is what he was looking for
all along.
              When John thinks what can't
be taken with us—how the table
is too much bulk for any wagon—the unspoken
skies of California, its unexplained ground
is what he wants. The travel.

John

May 9, 1851
Macune, Missouri

Each year the wheat is less his,
isn't grain enough, nor enough stalk
that he plows the plain world for.
The framed deed yellows
for how the light repeats itself
& John grows lean, pays out his days
as the old land's fare.
      And when
the rains don't come, when John reaches
in to turn a calf born later
bloodied, still, when emigrants raise the dust,
wave at us, just two days from St. Joe
& jump-off . . . then the plain stretches
in his mind, all the way to mountains
that bite back at thin air
& all that blue.
     When it snaps back fat
spilling free land, the room is swollen
with evening light & John jumps up,
mouth crowded with half-chewed food
& an idea.

May 18, 1851

Macune, Missouri

With his body he argues the power
of travel—the wheel of arms
rolls us, the perfect carriage
for two . . . & a matched pair
of horses run as if
there were no harness, no weight
whose follow never falters
for all the strides & pounding
hooves . . . the shadow
whose sun never moves.

Feeling the baby move

June 3, 1851
Macune, Missouri

I was a dance amongst myself
& led with my thickening body
a partner who knew the music
by heart. It was a song only
we could dance—the others
sat nodding & listened while under
the gazebo's white dome the musicians
performed in parts.
               Each one ponders
something small, something that makes
his fingers seem thick & clumsy.
But assembled, when the parts arrive
just in time, then they are playing,
& the song has found its dancer.

Portents

June 5, 1851
Macune, Missouri

I am to mind what I behold
for sake of the child that's in me,
attentions given to a world speaking
tongues of hawk flight,
crow-with-one-eye, the intrigue
of storm out of season, its wind
whose verge on singing veers
near then away from meaning, aloof
of all precaution.
                    Better
the tangle of the grasses
& the barn door's celebration
of its hinges with a clap.
Crow-with-one-eye hops
at the slant of his intentions
& flies away with the unfolding
of his shaggy wings.
                        Have it so—
my child will wink, have hair
the spring will muss for all my ribbons.
Little one dreams she flies
& Momma's the wind & the waking
before she falls. The wind
says I sing then
hey nonny & nonny & la.

Evidence

August 27, 1851
Macune, Missouri

John says, *It's darker & darker here,*
tearing off another hunk of bread,
making a meal of it. It is like all the loaves
I've ever baked or will, but for him
it is soured in thin light, from each detail
of his day the shining's been skimmed
like cream.
    The cow's dull eye
is evidence, the meager crop a witness
so simple it argues sing-song, rhymes *no*
with *go,* & when the field turns wily
it mutters *foe* into the wind.
      If I say
what I feel he'd hear it in tongues,
a warning against women carrying babies
turning in them. The evangelist's tent
was never fuller than John
in the stubbled field, John
filled with what moves him.

Bee for Helen's bridal quilt

September 15, 1851
Macune, Missouri

The afternoon was what she'd know
by wives & how we laughed—
all the while attending our work
without thinking it, as if it were another
heart the body would mind,
our fingers absorbed gathering
work we'd done alone, & woven
through it our stories who men
turned out to be.
                    In her happy fear
Helen put her hand on me
to feel the baby, & the baby obliged
with a good kick that made her start.
What a lively thing—& she ran
to her trunk abundant with quilts,
showed us she'd made ready,
had given years to the patterns
of the man she dreamed—& hadn't
we all?
          She spread them
in the sun, the future conjured
in calicos, muslin, occasional
velvet, spools & spools of thread
unwound & placed just so, each stitch
looming up on it, the waking.

Sara Adams Emblen
born October 27, 1851
Macune, Missouri

The midwife's hands blurred
in their cleaning & all the while
she gave direction, what she's repeated
til it's the path to the well
& you could fetch water at midnight
thinking only of the tea you'll make.
But then John was there with water
& complete she took to her own hands,
rubbed this birth away to join
the others—
    she held Sara's head
in those hands as I watched
it turn—like seeing hands guide
one crow into a current that carried it
gliding. Her hands spun away,
the wind picked up, in every direction
it howled carrying us the rest of the way.

Sara

November 9, 1851
Macune, Missouri

What is strange is in my arms,
the darkness I could not sleep in
came from me blue & shaking
with a cry above her size,
& though I had no milk for days
she sucked hard, tugged at the nipple,
& we were one animal
pulling itself along,
hearing its own labored breath
as the world's hummed coax to thrive.
We've travelled this way
two weeks & still

                there is nowhere to go
but into the splash of her iris,
the color of a tunnel that turns to light
where it opens again far away.

Snowfall

December 9, 1851
Macune, Missouri

It could be for him snow is
building like an orator, whose gestures
& rising voice suggest he's illumined
the entire sweep of field. And though
the wind argues where, each detail does
fall & is embraced as was revealed,
summing up a ground that reaches
inevitably for falling snow in
terms of snow . . .
                & John's every phrase
settles on Destiny as if a ground
clear for all the ways it's covered,
the nation, the nation of fathers in
their longing, the direction drifts lean
given the pull of wind.
                And Destiny
for detail will have people,
& they the dust of flour,
the kneading of my hands. I cut
one slice of bread, abide John
swallowing the dailiness settle
on what we must do, were made to do.

December 21, 1851

Macune, Missouri

Pity the poor fathers, their sons,
& how they go round, merry-go-round
without a song that conjures
their plodding to a dance.
Around & around, as if they'd straight
away arrive, & sing then the song
been earned, behind them all
their distance.
            Their very daughters
seem saved to them, born to sing it
far from gears that turn, & turn it
all around—not the stark thing bodied
& meshed, struck tooth by tooth
with whirling—invisible in that way
though it's what they see is missing,
the song, the song alone.

December 27, 1851

Macune, Missouri

She smiles as I swing
my hair across her face
& squints as if at light,
all my new weight of milk
pendulant—
& the planets, their moons,
surge through the heavens
given the simple pulse
of sun.
                    *

Sara is sudden squeals
& reaches for a stalk
of dusty light yoked
to a cloud's approach,
it looms above & ponders night—
then the sum of darkness
unveils constellations,
creatures of light.

December 29, 1851
Macune, Missouri

I give Sara a song
for her calming, then rock us
to just its time, we two
through darkness a bell
that nods a touch shy
of sounding, the congregation
already gathered.

January 2, 1852
Macune, Missouri

If a year were a field
our leaving's in this one selling
its magic elixir, sure-fire
distillation of all remedies
known to man.
             The clouds themselves
suffered the gout til they imbibed
in travel. And you, gentlemen,
think on it—you've seen
the bone-ache in the water being
frozen to a spot.
             The scoundrel's wit
is his playing to the humors
of an unsettled farmer—himself
a complicated joke, the laughter
in the lengths he'd go to get it.

Sara discovers her hand
January 10, 1852
Macune, Missouri

Columbus needed the travel,
his distance for the mood
to see new worlds within
the circle of his own—
less *they* make the crossing,
appearing one day naked
in the harbor, apparently
so startling the Queen
she'd forget her manners & shriek.

John in sleep

January 15, 1852
Macune, Missouri

The fields, the barn, all
things in rows or housed, squared
near as can to plumb, relax
in luxuries of error. The line
the horizon bends is slumber,
the well an ease of being
nearly straight as Father meant.
It's that draws John
to flight—because he'd fix it
he rises for the horizon's gesture,
its roundabout tease of longing.
Then several farms' sprawl makes just
one shape, but still it is familiar.
So higher & more, he begins to curve
into himself, like the ball he sees below—
all horizon, a sleek thing perfect,
something a boy might catch, or throw.

Grandmother's sampler
February 16, 1852
Macune, Missouri

Here are signs & wonders
one stitch at a time,
& the nine year girl saw
her hand flare up tethered
to each, the blue crewel yarn
slack or taut depending, just so
as the hand goes, like its echo,
like wind & where the leaves go.
The wind is you & carries you.
But then it's only an A
on the linen, sign the flurry subsides.
It's fine enough, but there.
Little wonder she'll name Mama
Alma, a small thing with her wind,
& cut the cord when the child looks
to her alone, eyes dense with blue.

The teacup she gave me as a child
February 17, 1852
Macune, Missouri

The stairs dipped palm deep
on either side given her steps past
reckoning, the flight made more
complex as the wood cupped,
the light it held in pools a form
of memory.
        Above she hovered
the landing, poised between
two windows' light, appearing
there the spirit of wood worn away,
how the hard lines curve in keeping
with their use.
        Grandmother
called to me, *Child & bring your cup,*
& those hours led me through
steps of my dowry's third quilt—
Think of it, this the pattern
he so admired—Jacob's Ladder
in blue, light blue, & white.

March 3, 1852
Macune, Missouri

I might as well blame the pump's
design on drawing water . . .
I swear the man's heart was wrought,
plunged when it was hot,
so fixed to shape & its
cool touch.
        But the machine
of raising dark waters
needs a mouth to sing them up—
else water is a mined chemical.
Or the sheer fluency is sucked out
as demonstration the contraption
works.
        Let the little handle be,
rusting in the rain. The hand of fit
has gone & left this sculpture,
its influence in my garden.
It could be enough
& in time the iron will deepens
my hydrangeas' blue.

Making ready

April 27, 1852
Macune, Missouri

I sang while I packed
as if I were in the woods, telling
the bear I'm on my way & mean
little, a bouquet, wildflowers
for the table.
        I topped the last crate
with a hymnal, put all those songs
in the dark with jars of seed,
forget-me-not & sweet pea,
one chopped clump of rose, roots
bound in burlap. I named them flute,
violin, drum.
        Then I remembered
my book of pressed flowers, the passenger
that prepared, lighter every day,
the hyacinth just a blue powder held
in place hovering above its stalk.
The voice.

My father 3 days before we leave
May 3, 1852
Macune, Missouri

As a young man he'd taken us his
far way, when I was a baby,
my mother the age I am now.
He told her then, *A grandfather
is an old man & that says it all.*
Kentucky & fathers that held him down
we rolled away. It was simple
travel, a line you could make
on a map.
   Now Papa's come back to it
wearing the mask of age
to hear the breath-like rightness of adventure
in a young man's hurried speech,
to hear the babbling of a baby girl
who tangles her hand in the mystery
of her grandfather's beard.
He must have promised silence
to be allowed to see this again.

The table, the apple, & the well

May 6, 1852
Macune, Missouri

I touch as memory touches
each thing that will remain, one finger
trailing off the table's edge,
feeling the table
                with that one.
Beneath the tree I hear each seed
hum the promise of ripeness, the host's
fall to earth, the recurrence a tune I carry
without a waste of space.
                     From the well
a call is moving toward its voice,
its face still the shimmer of a face.
I drop the bucket a last time, let it
go full, pull slow its poised weight,
lifting her out with the water
for one last cup of tea.

Departure
May 6, 1852

I looked for the first turn
of the wheel, something crucial to name
the start, as when I climbed a mountain
to find the river's first trickle down.
The blue of the wildflowers & the actual
mountain's loom brought me to the heart
of the matter. I was there with thistles
that wove me in, the mess the wind
made of my hair was the grasses'
pull across the slope. The idea I had flared
up with the hawk & was gone.
                             And so it was
John's bark for the oxen, a ladle
that fell from its hook, & Sara's shriek
at our assembling. For this beginning,
wherever it might be, I was the voice held
back in its throat, humming until I knew the words
the airs might need, a melody made for Sara
when she was inside me, without a name.

The preacher at St. Joe
May 9, 1852
St. Joe, Missouri

There was no confusing him
with the sinner who fell drink-heavy
near the front, there where the preacher pointed
down, finger shaking as if its blood
were lightning, with wrath for every meek
inch of earth it struck.
        That man
is no emigrant, brothers, sisters.
His soul has already settled, squatter's rights
in hell, he's got.
       Then that preacher
remembered gold, the tons of mud & gravel
he'd sluiced for a wealth of dust, the refined
heap a man can carry in one sack.
He puffed up, straining the seams,
he stomped the stage & sweat mightily,
but he couldn't bring that finger back
to poke his own little pile, he
couldn't shut up. And so, as I've
done before for so many men,
I was silent for him.

A saloon named Lil
May 9, 1852
St. Joe, Missouri

The story is the man lost her
as that is said, men & women
forgetful as they are
& possessed of meager vision.
Now his walls' refrain is their
several oils of Lil, his recollections
in gilt frames—each a relation
of how he remembered her
to an artist,
          each fittingly
wrong given what he chose to say,
errors he can cherish being
the only man who knows the correct
lips' fullness, how a blush
went down her neck & the shape
of that travel. Each right in manners
that intrigue him less—
          the style of her
favorite dress, a comb that held her hair.
Men toast the versions
& name them, each according to why
he drinks. The essence is now living
somewhere, without meaning.

The day we became the Barton Party

May 10, 1852
St. Joe, Missouri

Fifteen wagons found each other
& gathered outside of town, & while
I talked rice & flour, the men
chewed the weather, how wide
the Platte would be, being in town
long enough to know the issues.
And horses vs mules vs oxen
& weight & miles & time.
Then buffalo, buffalo—from them they leapt
to indians, to rifles & trails,
when snow might reach the Rockies,
one long moment settling
on the Donners.
        They were like a boy
throwing a ball against the barn at dusk,
& in the failing light the body's lamp
reaches to where the catch will be.
Then he throws hard to test it,
snares the bounding thing
at the last instant—or it leaps
past into the field & darkness
neither in nor out of the game.

May 10, 1852

St. Joe, Missouri

Then they settled into stories
& they made the fires dance.
A bottle in his hand, Barton
swore Nebraska's steep—
if they be neighborly the men
would show him kindness, ease
the labor of his oxen,
to drink & turn his wagon light.
I drank my brandy in tea as the oxen
nodded their blunt heads, their thanks
lolled in thick-tongued silence.
                    But the men,
their stories each a heave on the rope
men tie to what they want,
as they talked on & drank they would coil
Nebraska's length behind them. Now
they were all working together remembering
what they'd done when need be,
& near midnight, like a gigantic stump
in their field, the Rockies tore
loose & into view, approached
the pace the moon draws night.
Just a few more words, just
one more story . . .

Campfire

May 13, 1852
Nebraska

Do the flames skitter, sweet one?
& doesn't darkness attend them
exactly? If it had a mind
it would be to change it with grace.
Swaddling the fire, night is itself
transformed, it's shaped where it stoops,
bends to find itself rapt in
the other's every whim. Darkness
fusses about the fire like a mother
brushing her daughter's wisps of hair,
as a little wind slurs what's precise
in the mother's mind. There is a wind
that carries the smoke away
into the shapeless dark, where night
hasn't a mind to change.
It's yours, Sara. Your wind alone.

May 14, 1852
Nebraska

My feet in mud all day,
I don't feel in anything
at all, but set to,
a gate swung the full arc
back into the hasp & the line
of fence is whole.
            Leave the horses
out tonight, one day's plow
behind them, the next before,
& at the sides their masters dream
the fields full. Not a fence
they could jump, & where in the world
would they go?

Nebraska

May 25, 1852

I choose dust & ruts,
the wheel that rubs, the dry axle,
the spoke that dives for center.
I choose to do my own
breaking down. I'll put hoops
over my head, hitch a horse
to my hands & then drive me
hard for the New Start,
for Opportunity, Destiny, for Last
Chances & their bodies,
their lives that are carried west,
dragged & hauled, wheeled west,
led to a bedroll at night
by hands they dream
know the way.
         The sun
comes from where I came from
& sets where I will go.
Between: Nebraska, noon,
a moment when shadow
as I would choose it
waits beneath the wagon.

I choose to lose my milk
in sickness, a fever
that won't break til
the curdling's done. Sara. Sara.
To make the wagon light
I choose a wheel.

Grief

May 27, 1852
Nebraska

It folded its wings
to brood in me—
the tree that sings
when the wind blows,
cradle & all.

June 1, 1852
Nebraska

John divines loss as a task
of will, as if all this were
ceremony, the altar a nation wide.
I would smash the idols
& embrace the fulsome body—
less soon the sun depend
on us for rising, moon whisper
How full?
      Then find me
painted the earth's own red
chanting about the fire—
robed in feathers, I raise
the spirits, I fill the moon
until it bursts
& light spills & spills.

Seeing my sister

June 3, 1852
Platte River, South Fork

Across the Platte she waved
her bonnet, & the setting sun
behind her sent a shadow
over the slow water, each pass
of her arm a darkness crossed
over me, & then the red sun.
For a moment I thought it was rising,
that we were crossing to the other
side of things.
    But the sun did fall,
& between Lucy's shouts
I heard her baby cry, saw her dress splotch
dark with milk, & then she rushed
to their wagon.
    It can be pulled from you
just like that. Behind you
darkness has been gathering & you're wet
before you remember the milk
spills for that cry. Then you hurry
in your own time
while men linger over horses,
search out matches, & call
to you, calling your name long,
as if you were on the other side
of the river, as if calling
to the ferryman.

June 5, 1852

The wheels are the oxen's
dancers, the art of the bulk
as they progress—a grace
otherwise their heads suggest
nodding over food, at once
fluent & aloof as divining
wands—
        fork of hazel,
the keeper's hand is sure
to shake for provision
of his desire. What else
would he have but need
for the illusive—pushed
as he is by memory to daydream,
making it all seem real
with a shovel. I'd as soon love
the beast that provides the wheel.

June 6, 1852

Each step's a crumb
falling, unremarkable portion
of all, casual as what spills
from torn bread must,
the dust the accidents, a step
of eating,
   each step the balance
of leaving, the accident of arrival.
Where I've been birds line
all the way back feeding, each
smaller & smaller until one's
not there & I forget.
     Where they
poise they leave feathers,
each casual falling away spills
grays, white, a quiet blue—
a piece of sky as flight,
trace of their suspense.

Wagon upside down
June 7, 1852

Now if the wheel's to turn
it's by your hand, by your leave,
& feel the hub take to itself
the spokes' farthest reach—
what's meant about the heart.
There's friction you'd never know
but for the low rumble & grate.
That's the man slighted muttering
to himself, his plans to turn
his life around. Or turned round
but more—with your heart put into it
the spokes blur, rim & all hum
words of a tune I spun so
far away, silly, silly words—
but now the wheel's in air.
  Baby's got a raindrop
  right there on her chin.
  We've been inside all this day,
  who let that raindrop in?

June 8, 1852

He will arrive to the sea
as a man at the edge
of waking—who wonders
drowsed & slurred, swaddled
in remnants of his dreaming,
what it was brought him erect.
To gather shells, I'll say—
each little house of bone
another sign & wonder.
To see beyond
the farthest curve the point
of its departure—where that
murmur you hear is telling
& clear—you must needs smash it.
I'll make a basket
with my skirts & gather.
I shan't be smashing one.

June 9, 1852

A line from Missouri to the Rockies
runs through my heart & shakes,
a string drawn taut until it hums,
the song that trembles in my throat
when I cook or mend or wash
dishes in sand.
                    I dream
of dragging a bow across our trail,
playing a note so low John
puts his ear to the ground to hear it.
A horse, he says. *Or something about
to break the surface*
& still so far to go.

Buffalo
June 10, 1852

They return from the hunt not
as the men who had dreamed
buffalo until any cloud
was a notion of buffalo below,
gathering their desire & hovering
until the wind changed their minds—
& buffalo dispersed, letting form
go in a mixed wind.
                    Today
their yearning had not a cloud
& the sun beat its one hoof—
the men caught their dreaming
with running horses near death,
stormed buffalo & fired down
their thick bodies in drifts
& men made their weather.
Returning one dream less,
John carried by a horn its head.

Ecclesiastes
June 12, 1852

White hair to his shoulders,
a horseman came riding from sundown,
his only provisions dust & the Bible
he held aloft, held as a man can,
as if it had hold of him.
That preacher man
                    brought no news
but carried the word, delivered
on a voice that clapped thunder & let
lightning without time between.
For in the multitude of dreams and many words
there are also divers vanities.
                            And clap
the thunder, lightning shot from the god
he'd have flint, striking his mind across it.
I applied mine heart to know, and to search
and to know the wickedness of folly, even
of foolishness and madness. He raved so
you'd believe the stars were his flock.
But when we were rapt
he was finally plain, testified leaving
home we're fools—he turned on us
like the earth to its darkness.
                            Then we
were the darkness shot with light.
It was a mean thing he'd done,
they all said it, or It was just
words you must remember, & the men wanted
only to see what oxen might need,
women scoured wagons for mending,
& I am now beside the lamp.

June 13, 1852

The fool foldeth his hands together,
and eateth his own flesh.
Ecclesiastes

If I hold to loss, encircle
with my arms, I'd crush it,
burst the fragile skin
of what remains, memory's white
powdered belly—& out jump
me bedeviled.
     I will cling
to a single hair it won't miss,
witness loss spin
beneath the moon. The wheel of it,
the carriage, the rider who
sings from the dark.

June 14, 1852

All the rivers run into the sea
yet the sea is not full.
       Ecclesiastes

Where will John's sons go
with the earth plowed straight & cropped—
a nation wide behind them settled
for placid abundance.
                    If I might raise
one enduring man . . . his weight
could tip the continent & tumble
generations in a clatter by his porch.
Ezra there had a longing, I'd say,
& short-lived wives. He fancied
God's will moved him, though I swear
it was a horse.
                    I'd grow shrill
soon enough, my delivery
a claw sharpened by its work.
Woman, rip these years & shred them,
their tatters will seem to him
the very fabric of a man.

June 15, 1852
Ft. Laramie

The fortress of his dream
is the world as it relents
to his impressions
& holds them for a spell—
wagon tracks, a mound of earth
& it the cross, the scar
across his stronger hand—
earnings in the tender
of arrival.
        Why else lug
the bison's head & raise it
by its horns, but that it reminds
his desire is substantial—
& didn't the creature run
as if it knew his mind?
Good or bad makes no matter,
instead it all has meaning—
a stronghold of such size
one can't tell if more's
held out or in.

At Ft. Laramie
June 17, 1852

I counted sacks of flour,
tugging the seams looking for strength
& I wondered how far the rice would go.
John said we only need food to get there.
Tending to these things makes loving
the man in my arms at night like eating,
the surplus & the wanting, the growl
of a stomach that won't stop working
though empty of all but its own juice.

For each thing the wagon can't hold,
for each thing abandoned to ease
the oxen's pull, my mind swells
to hold that much more. In this world
there is something wrong with love,
as its weight is what's wrong with the
china closet we left behind.
We placed it facing east as I insisted,
between the ruts. Let the next train roll
through its doors. I opened them wide
& thought of every yes I'd ever said to John.

June 21, 1852

If there was cream to churn
I'd remember butter in my arms
& a song to work in, lift & fall
through my work as it thickens, until
I'd transformed it wholly—
like the last month I carried
Sara, giving it all my weight.
Then I'd think of bread, knead
the dough, turning it into itself
with a lean, lift on my toes a dance
of weight, cover & rise, shape
the stubbed shape, cover & rise—
all to spread the butter on,
watch it melt back thin, taste
its being butter now, the cream
far behind. But it would melt
by itself here.
                    It would pool its fat
& slide, the casual chore of a heat
that smudges the hard line of the flats
with shimmer & blur. Each day we stalk
a curtain that waves & waves before us.
On the other side John sees rock-sure
the new start awaits us, our arrival
another child, pet of the new start.
John churns in me to make it so—
a son, he says, hurrying to him & the way
he'll tell him this as story.

Born in 1947, Richard Speakes was raised in a family that lived in several states during his childhood, including Washington, Virginia, Rhode Island, California, and Alaska. He thinks with equal affection of Seattle, Washington, and Santa Rosa, California, and so has at least two homes. With his wife Judy Appel and their two daughters, he now lives in New Orleans, where he teaches at the University of New Orleans as an instructor in its English Department.

He received an M.A. in Creative Writing in 1980 from the University of Washington, where he studied with the poets David Wagoner, William Matthews, Richard Blessing, and Jane Shore. While at the University of Washington he was for two years the Managing Editor of **The Seattle Review**. Speakes' most significant training has come from a long apprenticeship to the poet, translator, editor, and teacher, D. L. Emblen. With Emblen and the poet Richard Welin, Speakes edited **Loon, A Journal of Poetry** during its six years of publication, 1973-1978. Through association with Emblen and Welin, Speakes began to learn his craft, a learning he cherishes all the more because it had no established hours, no degrees, no goals beyond its own relentless and loving activity.

Speakes, who in 1979 had a chapbook, **Necessities**, published by Clamshell Press of Santa Rosa, California, is currently working on a second book of poems (whose working title is **Lies That Forgive the Truth**) and thinking it would be interesting to write prose-fiction.

Ahsahta Press

POETRY OF THE WEST

MODERN

*Norman Macleod, *Selected Poems*
 Gwendolen Haste, *Selected Poems*
*Peggy Pond Church, *New & Selected Poems*
 Haniel Long, *My Seasons*
 H. L. Davis, *Selected Poems*
*Hildegarde Flanner, *The Hearkening Eye*
 Genevieve Taggard, *To the Natural World*
 Hazel Hall, *Selected Poems*
 Women Poets of the West: An Anthology
*Thomas Hornsby Ferril, *Anvil of Roses*
*Judson Crews, *The Clock of Moss*

CONTEMPORARY

*Marnie Walsh, *A Taste of the Knife*
*Robert Krieger, *Headlands, Rising*
 Richard Blessing, *Winter Constellations*
*Carolyne Wright, *Stealing the Children*
 Charley John Greasybear, *Songs*
*Conger Beasley, Jr., *Over DeSoto's Bones*
*Susan Strayer Deal, *No Moving Parts*
*Gretel Ehrlich, *To Touch the Water*
*Leo Romero, *Agua Negra*
*David Baker, *Laws of the Land*
*Richard Speakes, *Hannah's Travel*

*Selections from these volumes, read by their authors, are now available on *The Ahsahta Cassette Sampler.*